"...the humor is timely, the examples are real."
—Mary Napoletano, Rochester, MN

"Insightful and thought provoking in its message,
Straight Talk *is grounded in basic values applicable to*
many of life's surprises."
—Sharon Snyder,
former elementary school principal

"...an extremely well written book about life's realities...."
—Jean L. Boomhower

"Karel's sense of humor will brighten your day!"
—Kelly McDonald,
Blue River Community College

"I felt like I was reading a family diary that had been
left behind. ...filled with delicious stories and useful
advice for everyday living, this book is one to have
around to feed your mind, body and soul."
—Susan M. Hutchinson,
Licensed Funeral Director

"Laugh and learn with Karel and K.C.'s sincere insight
into self-examination, introspection and provocative
ideas to build your self-esteem."
—Betty L. Burley, English Teacher

STRAIGHT
TALK

STRAIGHT TALK

Getting off the Curb

Karel Murray and K.C. Lundberg

arnica
PUBLISHING, INC.

Portland, Oregon

Library of Congress Cataloging-in-Publication Data

Murray, Karel, 1954-
    Straight talk : getting off the curb / by Karel Murray and K.C.
Lundberg.
      p. cm.
    ISBN 0-9726535-0-3 (pbk. : alk. paper)
    1. Conduct of life. I. Lundberg, K.C., 1948- II. Title

BF637.C5M87 2003
158.1--dc21

                        2003002614

Arnica Publishing
620 SW Main, Suite 345
Portland, OR 97205

Table of Contents

ACCOUNTABILITY

BE PROACTIVE

MAKE THE BEST OF THINGS, COME WHAT MAY

Authors' Note

With the frustration of the non-productive office water cooler sessions and coffee gossip conferences, we concluded that someone should stand up and advocate accountability. Amidst the dissolution of the core family, lowering of self-esteem, and the evasion of personal responsibility, we felt the need to call individuals into action, not resignation.

Sitting around complaining about or avoiding issues was not how we were raised. Our parents inspired us to step forward and throw our hats into the ring. Choices confront us every day.

With this book we hope to impact your lives with a shove of encouragement to join us on the journey to accountability.

Knock. Knock.

Morning dawn burst into the office dining area, unaffected by the darkened glass windows. The cafeteria tabletops gleamed, reflecting the warm sunlight. The bittersweet smell of freshly brewed coffee drifted through the quiet room, and I smiled, grateful for another quiet Monday.

I hoped this peaceful moment would set the pattern for the rest of my day. Often, I face an assault of administrative questions or employees' requests for instructions on processing priorities, leaving me feeling overwhelmed.

As I leaned against a counter, in relaxed contemplation, I detected a faint sigh. I quickly surveyed the area, attempting to locate the source of the soulful sound. Nearby, I heard another mournful exhale. A muffled murmur directed my attention to a commercial refrigerator. The wastebin, which typically occupied a spot next to the fridge, stood askew from the wall. Overcome with curiosity and concern, I advanced towards it and found one of my clerks huddling next to the wall and the refrigerator behind the bin, rocking back and forth in a fetal position. An involuntary gasp left my lips as I knelt down to help her.

I extended the palm of my hand to her tear-stained cheek and asked if I could help. Looking up, she searched my face for signs of disapproval and desperately grasped my wrist, anchoring it to her cheek. Observing her silence and body language, I inquired if she had taken any pills and, if so, what kind. Slurring, she replied, "A bottle of sleeping pills. I just need to rest...I'm tired of being me."

Gently, I asked her if she'd rather curl up on a warm couch instead of the cold vinyl floor. With her hesitant nod, I slowly drew her up and guided her to my office, whereupon I called for medical assistance.

In just a few short minutes, the secure, pragmatic world I had known ground to a halt. Shocked, I realized that all I had observed in the past had no definition. I had only noticed the fragile masked surfaces of people's entities.

Knock. Knock. Who am I? Who are you? What a wake up call! I had drifted through life unaware of the many layers that develop a human existence. At that definitive point, I realized that an abundance of understanding waited behind the Cheshire Cat's grin. We need to nourish our ability to break through the surface and genuinely comprehend what motivates those around us to work, play or simply exist in their environment.

Why? So we can begin to consider our own roles in human interaction. Understanding others gives us a deeper sense of ourselves. The games we choose to play affect our decisions. As adults, our child-hood contests evolve into word and mental games. Sometimes others don't play by the rules.

Having lived in geographically diversified segments of the United States, I've noticed a distinct change of gears in terms of how people conduct their lives. Generally, though, I've noticed an overall lowering of self-confidence and personal pride and an unwillingness to step out of the crowd. My observations reveal that people long to be noticed, but they see the drawbacks to standing out before they see the freedom it offers.

That forlorn clerk retreated into herself and attempted to end her life. She lacked the tools and support to step out of the crowd and shout for help. Instead, she withdrew and hid from her peers. Her silent cry shouted at me to stop and pay attention. I cringe to think what might have happened if I had altered my schedule that day. That stocky little clerk couldn't create a comfortable path that would deliver her from her problems or carry her to a haven of help.

This forty-year-old employee, living with her overbearing elderly mother, never married or even came close to establishing a dating relationship. Her self esteem tanked. A sense of purpose derived from her work allowed the opportunity to hide in a cubicle. She put in her eight hours, making herself a virtual island within the company. She displaced herself from all interaction, except what was necessary for her to maintain her position. Unfortunately, her self-imposed isolation built an insurmountable barricade, which entrenched her so deeply that suicide presented itself as her only viable escape hatch.

Why should you spend your valuable time with me? What could I possibly have to offer you? I'm not famous, nor do I have a doctorate in social behavior or psychology. I extend to you an ordinary person's perspective, a first-hand view of life. As a sales clerk, bank teller, farmer, mother, secretary, claims examiner, supervisor, regional manager, realtor, real estate broker manager, trainer and national motivational speaker, I humbly offer my experiences and perceptions to give insight and inspiration.

My advice comes in the form of stories based on my life experiences. We all have such moments of insight, but often fail to learn from or even remember them. Our past interactions act as our teachers, and we need to remember that more often. Only then can we evolve into students of life. It is time for you to stop, reflect and learn from your own experiences.

Who are you? As you look in the mirror, who do you see? Who do you *want* to see? Do you see a person who finds passion in everyday events? Have you become dulled to the hard knocks of life and no longer find joy in anything?

As a committed player, I'll ask you not to be skeptical and turn your back on taking an honest, critical look at yourself. Please read the following stories with an open mind, and hopefully, one will strike a chord and lead to positive introspection and action.

SELF-IMAGE

Sweat Pants of Life

Somewhere along the line, we got our priorities screwed up. Who determined I had to conform to trendsetter designer looks, and why do I live in fear of the fashion police?

Getting ready to go out in public is a formalized ritual for me. The process, methodical and precise, with each step designed to create a "look" that enhances my best qualities, continues as a daily challenge. It's hard to celebrate a sharp wit through cosmetics.

For thirty or more years, I have carefully applied my makeup, from foundation to mascara, building each layer cautiously and fastidiously, along with styling my short, sun-bleached (through the magic of chemicals) hair with a blow dryer and curling iron. Each morning, I narrowly miss suffering first degree burns of the forehead as I work on an errant lock of hair. The end result is held firmly in place with a light mist of hair spray amidst fits of sneezing.

Next, I face the arduous task of selecting what to wear for the day. How problematic this is depends completely upon my mood and how much water my body has retained. My "professional" clothing (designed to inspire confidence in my management and sales ability) has slimming lines and unforgiving, rigid waistbands—the designers once again dictating that my figure conform to their expectations. God forbid a generous waist should grace their creation....

Well, they're out of luck. Each water retention day, I send a blessing to the inventor of the safety pin. Linking two pins together, end-to-end, I can just ease out the waistband, hiding the transgression under a jacket. A close look at the silk tank top reveals a small coffee stain dead front and center. No problem. Put it on backwards and no one will be the wiser. I just have to remember not to take my jacket off during the day.

The final phase involves jewelry and shoe selection. Having a generous supply of each does not make the task easier. When regarding the jewelry, I ask myself, "Do I feel like wearing accessories today?" "How about sharpening the look with square silver earnings, a belt buckle and lapel pin...nope." The softly rounded necklace slide, bangle watch and long accenting scarf win the accessory decision.

Decisions on how to tie the scarf ultimately overwhelm me. How to get the slippery silk piece in place and make it stay put requires an extreme amount of patience and creativity. I end up with a long skinny scarf draped over my shoulders and looped under my jacket lapel. I tie the ends off into loose knots. Not bad....

Locating the shoes that complement the look I'm trying to achieve will complete my ensemble. Closed or open-toed? High, medium or low heel? Contrasting or conforming color? Strap, tie or slip on? I rule out three pair due to the body bloat which seems to have spread to my feet. My final decision guides the medium heel, fake alligator pump towards my waiting foot.

Forgot the panty hose....

Pulling the skirt up over my hips, the safety pins pop open. Luckily, they didn't draw blood. The day is starting to look up. I tear open the new hosiery pouch with my teeth, smearing lipstick over the wrapping. Luckily, I avoid getting lipstick on the hose. Another victory....

More water retention than I thought. My feet slide in all right, but it's a whole other story getting the hosiery up over my thighs and hips. I lay on top of the bed, my feet airborne, and use gravity and upper arm strength to position my support hose.

Starting to sweat now....

Nylons firmly in place, I slide the skirt back down my hips, reset the pins and try to stuff my "extra" waist back inside the waistband. Have you ever sat down and felt your stomach hit your thighs? Startled me the first time it happened. I thought something fell out and I hadn't noticed. Kind of like after you have your first baby and they forget to tell you that all that stretched skin won't just suck right back into place. You're left with a bowl of jiggly stomach with nowhere to go.

"Surprise," it yells, "I'm back!"

I look in the mirror and realize it is the best it is going to get. The color seems to complement my skin, and the look is fairly trim. Everything can't be perfect can it? Holding in my stomach, I can almost imagine what I looked like thirty pounds ago.

Almost. Maybe if I shut my eyes to half-mast and look sideways. There. Better.

Off to work, ready to take on the world. So what if I can't breathe? I can do that later.

My panty hose are so tight my legs want to spring upwards with each step. I look like a circus horse counting to ten. The scarf decides to have a life of its own. The loose knotted ends snag on latch lever door handles, bringing me off my feet to a sudden stop. Ever sit on your scarf and have your chin pulled down to the desktop? You just pray it doesn't happen in front of people.

Throughout the day, I dread the eventual use of the rest room. If anything gives out....

On the drive home, all I can think about is changing into my sweat pants. You know, the ones with the matching sweatshirt. Just the right color that cat hair doesn't show in bright light and food stains are camouflaged by the design. My husband holds them out to me as I stumble through the door tearing the scarf from my neck and flinging it on the floor.

What took forty-five minutes to put on is stripped from my body in one minute flat. I glide into my welcoming sweat pants and sigh. I'm home.

• • • • •

My sweat pants are a life lesson. I see people immaculately dressed for their "career presentations." However, I also marvel when they reveal their preferred persona while relaxing in their own version of my sweat pants.

My husband's grandfather, a self-made man, had the right idea. He owned four outfits. Period. All exactly the same. White undershirt, khaki shirt, khaki pants, brown belt and brown shoes. The only variation was the location of the burn holes from his cigar ash. If forced to, he would wear his only black suit to weddings and funerals.

He faced the world with an attitude of "here I am...take it or leave it." And they took him. No problem.

So, I've decided to live his philosophy. No more conforming to an ideal public image that just isn't me. Simply put, I'm putting on the sweat pants of my life and going forward into the world.

Where are yours?

Hall of Mirrors

A while back, I gained some unwanted weight and went up two clothing sizes. Frankly, I didn't like looking at my reflection. One morning, while dressing for work in the bathroom, I turned around to check my hemline and discovered that I didn't recognize the rear in the mirror! My mental image of my body did not match reality. And only until I acknowledged the truth could I make the decision to do something about it or accept it as it stood (or sat, if you will).

As my early childhood slowly fades to memories, adulthood steps in to play its role. Reality checks, like my revelation in the mirror, are an integral part of the journey to self awareness. I attempt to relate real-life stories because we all have them, and we should tuck them away as a cache of learning tools. While life experiences can be both hilarious and depressing, they also carry with them a certain wisdom that may be useful in future situations.

· · · · ·

Do you remember the lineups in elementary school when it was time to file in order of the tallest to the shortest? No matter what the criteria, I always stood at the front of the line. As a child, I thought having a tall stature was fun. But as I advanced into my teens, it got old quickly. Somehow, this was not my idea of being at the top of the class.

I soon found that life would always place barriers like this one in my path. Not only was I tall, but *noticeably* tall for my age and gender. My twin brother, who stood over six feet tall by seventh grade, was the lucky one. Kevin, the tall, dark, handsome boy who played center position in basketball, easily attracted the opposite sex.

Society perceived Kevin's height as a positive. From his perspective, though, it was a negative. College students bullied Kevin while hanging out at our neighborhood park. They assumed, due to his extreme height, he could only be a college student. Kevin's lack of coordination and maturity made him an easy mark for ridicule.

I had always assumed that Kevin enjoyed his stature. Wrong! Maybe if we'd joined forces, we could have confronted his problems by collaborating instead of isolating ourselves and leaving us to handle our own challenges without a support system.

If Kevin had only shared with our parents his fear and lack of understanding of his continual assaults by "mature" and older kids, he would have received solutions to alleviate his predicament. At the bare minimum, he could have been counseled in dealing with others' perceptions of his physical acceleration, which in turn would provide better coping mechanisms.

• • • • •

Listening to demo records from the radio station my dad worked for introduced me to all styles of music. I'd sing and dance to polkas, rock' n' roll or classical music, putting my imagination in full 45 RPM. Not only did I dance, but I dressed up in all the can-cans I could grab from my three sisters' dresser drawers, trying to copy the lovely tutus of *Swan Lake*. As the ballerina, I waited in the wings for my entrance—tall, composed and fluffy! Mom, my ardent supporter, observed this creative display of artistry and encouraged me to take ballet lessons.

In retrospect, I believe Mom had an ulterior motive in getting me to vent my passion for dancing at a local studio. At home we had a huge picture window in the living room draped with translucent curtains. As a young, aspiring ballerina, I unknowingly provided the neighborhood with nightly variety shows.

I delighted in my ballet lessons. I could wear costumes with make-up and dance my heart out. I not only looked like a snow swan, I became one. Toes tracing the five standing positions fluidly, knees bending smoothly, arm movements arching over my head...I gave it my all.

And it appeared that my mother's plan worked! As I grew taller, I became more graceful. By seventh grade, at 5'8" tall and 135 pounds, I towered over my peers and outweighed them all. While I danced, I forgot about my height.

My instructor, short, petite with dyed blonde crispy hair, wore colorful scarves draped around her neck, accentuating her matching leotard. With wizened skin, elegant long fingers, and flowing gestures, Mrs. Renaldo instructed her charges as a force of nature.

One day, clapping her hands loudly, she announced, "We must prepare for the seventh grade recital! Girls—quiet!" Pointing at me, she declared, "Karel! You will have the honor of ending the show by performing the Grand *Jeté!* You will soar through the air into...."

Distracted, she ordered my classmates, small giggling sprites, to pay attention to the proper order of the dance sequence.

"I close the show? With the Grand *Jeté?* REALLY?" I stammered.

"Yes. In fact, I'm planning on having a young man catch you at the end!"

"Not Earl!" I yelped.

I peered down at him. Earl stood at least four inches shorter and weighed at least sixty-five pounds less than I. Wearing his hair plastered to his head, Earl had a nervous habit of continually adjusting his glasses on his sweaty nose.

But, I admit, he could tap. His feet pounded out staccato rhythms unparalleled by any other in the class.

Earl smiled uncertainly up at me. A flicker of fear passed over his face.

Mrs. Renaldo brushed off my concerns quickly, "No. Not Earl...we have Steve lined up to catch you at the end. He's a high-school senior—strong enough to catch you easily. He plays football, you know! His mother owes me a favor and Steve is willing to do this as long as he doesn't have to wear tights." Relief surged through me.

Steve arrived at the next class—tall, muscular, displaying exactly the kind of manly arms I wanted to leap into. I even managed to drape my arms delicately around his neck when he caught me. My heart fluttered. He just smiled and gently set me down. Every time. He acted as if I were light as a feather.

We practiced our hearts out. The Big Night came almost too quickly. Parents filled the theater—standing room only—and watched in delight the end result of all that expense for the fairy-like costumes.

Dance sequences flew by in a blur. Then, moved to my end of the stage, I prepared for my finale…the grand leap across the stage into Steve's arms.

I lifted my head high, arched my neck in a swan-like fashion, took a deep breath and began the leap of my life—exactly on cue. As envisioned by Mrs. Renaldo, I soared up into the air. I turned my head toward Steve, a large smile beaming from my face.

Only, there was no Steve….

Earl stood there with his bony arms out-stretched, small legs quaking and eyes wide open in terror. Steve had been injured at football prac-tice, which necessitated that Earl, being the only male available, replace him. Mrs. Renaldo, in her wisdom, did not forewarn me, as she felt it would impact my ability to perform an elegant Grand *Jeté*. It was the finale after all!

My smile turned into a silent scream.

Plunging downward, my leading knee burst past Earl's waiting arms and plowed right into his solar plexus.

"OOOOPH!" Air rushed out of his little lungs as we slammed onto the stage. My high velocity momentum slid us across the chalky floor into the back stage area. A collective groan erupted from the audience followed by a respectful silence. Tentative clapping began soon after.

Gasping, Earl eased me to the side, wincing as he held his ribs. Ever the performer, he stumbled out onto the stage. Looking regally over the crowd, he gestured for me to join him. I did, and we took our bows.

The audience went wild. A glorious moment.

At the end of the recital, after the crowds had dispersed, Mrs. Renaldo drew me aside, guiding me by the shoulders to a nearby bench. She assumed the authority stance for a moment and then declared, "Karel, you'll never perform as a ballerina. You're just too tall." Those simple and direct words broke my heart. No more tutus for me.

My vision of Carnegie Hall in New York crumbled. I would never dance *Swan Lake* as the lead—or even perform in the chorus line.

* * * * *

The horrible word "reality" steps into our existence more often than we'd like and blares at us, "You can't do that anymore!" It steers us to paths we hadn't planned on traveling.

Past experiences outline our moves, and we recognize that life isn't always fair. As we advance through life, we bump into things—egos, rules, hurdles and other barriers. We learn from the black and blues of life. Bruises fade over time, but hopefully leave impressions of what not to do the next time. We need to adjust and direct energy to areas we can thrive in.

We need to take an objective look at ourselves on a regular basis and see if we have caused our tribulations. Look hard in your hall of mirrors, select the reflection you can accept and work with it. We can only correct a problem once we have identified it. Admitting our mistakes gives us the courage to advance along the game board.

It all comes down to whether or not you like yourself. All your perceived flaws—cellulite, stretch marks, wrinkles, flab, lack of control, addictions or social ineptitudes—can shatter a positive self-image into shards. Success and competence will seem unattainable if you deem yourself unworthy of respect. You are your own garbage bin. No one is allowed to root around inside, unless you let them. That includes you. Dump your perceived imperfections in the garbage and slam the lid shut.

Dog at a Dance

I went on my first date in tenth grade. He stood over six feet tall, was a senior and was considered the school "hood." Glenn wore a letter jacket, had long frizzy hair and rolled Camels in his shirt-sleeve—he was a Brando, one of the wild ones. According to the high-school rumor mill, he had a long list of conquests.

I usually intimidated the opposite sex because of my height and my status as the mayor's daughter. I embodied the stereotypical wallflower at teen dances. You'd think with aching feet from continually holding up the wall, I would have learned not to set myself up for failure. But then a miracle occurred; Glenn asked me out to the teen dance. I leapt at the offer. A dance? With a guy taller than me? My loneliness overwhelmed my common sense. The dance awaited my debut.

Saturday night, as my date pulled up to the house, I raced to the car before he could even shift into park. As he drove me to the dance, I neared a state of hyperventilation as I pictured myself dancing with him. I thought about all my classmates envying me and how I finally had the chance to show off all those dance moves I had studied for so long.

While engaged in my incredible first dance, Glenn's buddy tapped him on the shoulder and asked, "Whadyah doin' here with that dog?" Who was he talking about? I thought I looked great. This cruel remark echoed in the air. My date scowled, "I know she doesn't look like much, but she's got a nice personality." His buddy pointed out that he thought Glenn was too cool to be hanging around with someone like me. With that statement, my dance partner said, "You're right!" He shoved me away, leaving me there to pick up whatever survived of my pride.

Without a word, I left the dance floor and walked home. As I hunched over in the winter wind, with the snow slipping into my new shoes, all I could think about was that I had been publicly rejected by a no-good hood. By the time I arrived at my doorstep, I had convinced myself that there really was something wrong with me. The perception of my date's friend had transferred to Glenn (peer pressure) and I became the brunt of that perception. My fragile teen self-image had been shattered. From that day forth, nothing I wore looked good—whether it was make-up or clothes or anything else.

A hood had rejected me.

I found it hard to look my peers in the eyes, feeling the sting of public humiliation all around me. A lot of damage for a first dance. I did it to myself; it was an accident waiting to happen.

· · · · ·

Rejection comes in varied forms—it can blind-side us. It unveils itself with varying degrees of intent, resulting in emotional hurt because we present some kind of threat.

We can become a threat to others just by walking into unknown territory. We simply want to do well. In a new job or at a party, we seek a level of comfort and acceptance. But sometimes, if we display confidence, knowledge, assertiveness, savvy and autonomy, the natives can have a natural tendency to challenge us. They initiate efforts to displace us in order to protect their "perceived" superior position. They are intimidated by our mere presence and their self preservation kicks in. Survival of the fittest. Consider two rams locking horns…except people don't lock horns—they reject. Not fulfilling our promise or obligation, a misunderstanding or a simple lack of communication may result in rejection.

Regardless of the form it takes, our greatest fear is centered around the mortification of having others witness our rejection. We pray it doesn't occur in front of others. Unfortunately, rejection has a way of finding a public arena in which to present itself. The idea that our actions or decisions are being discussed by others over coffee or on the phone hovers over our mental well-being. We experience it as memories of peer pressure. Ultimately, this feeling of inadequacy and embarrassment invades our everyday lives.

The type of emotional upheaval I experienced at the dance can drive people to run home, crawl into bed and throw the covers over their heads. Why do we allow others to determine our self-esteem?

Shame on us.

No one has the power to make us unhappy unless we permit it. So again, why do we allow it?

Don't give up if you collide with rejection. Try not to take it personally. Yes, we all have human frailties, and we will take rejection personally, but I encourage you to try and step back and analyze the situation objectively. Look for ways to make rejection work to your advantage.

Understand the "animal" you are interacting with. Do your research. Determine the motivation: social/economic background, family culture, education level and level of tolerance for change. As long as you understand the "animal" you can work around it. This eliminates blindsided reactions.

Picture this: you come upon a rattlesnake ready to strike. You think you're a goner. But let's back up. You have entered the enemy's territory. Pay attention to the warning signs. Intimidating questions, impatience, type of eye contact, curtness or aggressive body language. Are the wagons circled and are you on the outside? Be ready to protect yourself.

You can run.

* * * * *

Could it be we prefer to perceive life through rose-colored glasses? Our parents stepped on ours by introducing reality into our fantasies.

Mom firmly advised us to stand up for our rights. My older sister, K.C., had the opportunity to put Mom's advice to the test when she found herself hurriedly walking home from school with an unwelcome escort shadowing her—a taunting classmate. He teased her relentlessly day in and day out. I overheard Mom counseling her that this was the third grader's way of showing affection. Affection? My sister decided to ignore her own personal take on the situation and took Mom's advice, which was to stand up for herself and face him man to man...well, girl to boy.

One afternoon, K.C. had enough of his "affection." She wasn't going to let him bully her anymore. She spun on her heels and struck him on the cheek. It landed as a light slap, a feeble attempt for the first time, but she connected...and so did he! He slapped her right back! Mom hadn't covered this situation, so K.C. ran like hell.

Live life like a youngster. Instead of avoiding confrontation, why not face it nose to nose, opening yourself to a bit of bruising? K.C. had not reviewed all the possible responses to her action, which was her only pitfall. We seek advice from others in order to arrive at a solution which benefits us. K.C. learned that when she strikes out, she should anticipate a counter strike—a simple childhood lesson applicable to corporate politics, or just plain human interaction.

Breaking the glass ceiling is a common fear. To attempt to shatter a corporate barrier designed to protect traditions, perceptions, politics, procedures and attitudes is daunting. You may avoid striving for promotions because of concerns about the consequences of tapping on the glass. Recommendations for improved performance gather dust in file folders due to lack of confidence and action. Excess energy is expended in protecting your turf rather than in moving your career forward.

Understand that positive and negative consequences exist. When getting ready for the corporate tap on the glass, ask yourself, "What's the worst and the best reaction that could present itself?" By placing all scenarios on the table, you can ready yourself more easily to react to any counterstrike. The key is preparation.

Examine the event and determine whether it will make a difference to you in the future. Accept it or reject it. But, move on!

When do we wake up? What does it take to make us understand that we orchestrate how a situation unfolds? We do have some control.

In order to deal rationally with rejection, don't underestimate the importance of attitude. We don't always get what we want. Keep that in mind. In fact, we may never get what we feel we deserve, but it's how we, ourselves, perceive the situation that really counts.

Does rejection occur for a reason? I believe it does. We need to examine why it happens. For example, have we placed our goals so high that they extend beyond our reach, thus ensuring that rejection is inevitable? By overreaching our grasp and failing continually, we confirm our low opinion of ourselves. Rejections, however, can lead to positive outcomes.

Don't let others totally dictate your nature, success or what timeline you follow.

Stop playing the victim and rerunning the self-hate tapes in your subconscious. Quit counting your deficiencies when you should shout about your strengths. A sound, positive self-image is the greatest gift you'll give to yourself, friends, family and community.

SOCIALIZATION

So What if Everyone Else Is Doing It?

Be true to yourself. This may be considered an overused adage, but I disagree. Dealing with peer pressure starts at early stages of life. I recall my son, Ben, as a toddler, suffering the loneliness of isolation as the neighborhood golden circle kept him out of their embrace. In fact, the adults wouldn't socialize with us despite our efforts to introduce ourselves. As newcomers, I guess we didn't fit the neighborhood criteria.

Sometimes we focus so much on the drawbacks of action that we fail to focus on the rewards of nonconformity. Often, children lead with their hearts. As an example, one morning on the school bus a group of unruly students were loudly taunting the physical and mental characteristics of my nephew's friend.

Marcus, my nephew, got up and stepped into the bus aisle to defend his good friend. He stood up and stepped out of the crowd. He took a leap of faith, challenged the busload of kids and supported his friend, not concerned with his well-being. His bold action was greeted by an awed silence.

Unaware that he had placed himself at risk with his schoolmates, Marcus made his choice.

· · · · ·

This child's simple but rare gesture is applicable to a neighborhood chat session or the professional arena. Have you faced a situation in which you've felt that the conversation veered to an inappropriate level or where peers treated others unfairly? How did you handle it? Did you sit back and watch instead of becoming involved?

You have choices you need to make before taking the appropriate action. Sometimes you have to make spontaneous decisions because the chance to react may be forever lost. Define who you are and what you believe. That in turn will dictate how you react to situations and how others conduct themselves in your presence. Peer pressure has an obvious form and process. It is the ultimate team sport. Consider my observations:

PLAYING THE GAME

You don't need to conform. You recognize the leader and the decision-maker. Understand the job description and how it defines your place in the pecking order. This applies to your career as well as your home and social life. Show them how your desired position would be enhanced by your uniqueness. The leader may want to pigeon-hole you into a specific job description. It's your decision to accept or reject the position based upon the terms offered.

If the role is a critical one for your future success, you may consider taking on the opportunity as offered and begin to work within the system. As you learn the ropes and earn respect, you can then determine ways to redefine the guidelines to more closely align with your expectations and needs.

MEMBERSHIP NOT ALLOWED IF DEEMED UNACCEPTABLE

You + no rules = unacceptability. A clique demands that the member agrees to place the well-being of the group ahead of individual beliefs or ideas. As an individual, you can decide to submit to the group mentality or keep searching for a better fit.

FIND THE LEADER

When you join a group, locate the leader or trendsetter by identifying the person who possesses the strength and charisma that determines how a peer group develops. Successful leadership requires constant modification and growth to retain vitality and viability.

Pressure may erupt when you start developing and expressing your own ideas, deviating from the leader's objective. At this point, you must decide if you should create a new group or try to dominate the old one.

THE GROUP REFLECTS YOU

As a child, do you remember how your parents attempted to set parameters of acceptability and how they worked continually to steer you towards groups that reflected your family values? Your character is judged by those with whom you associate. Pick carefully.

INDIVIDUALS MODIFY PEER PRESSURE

Unconditional acceptance by the group means you face setting aside your identity or proving to them your value as a unique individual worth inclusion. My son, Ben, wanted to fit into his peer group's dynamics by establishing an attitude where he'd do anything to achieve acceptance, until the group collided with his value system. To maintain his inherent ethics, he carefully voiced his objections. Ben finally refused to accept the promoted mentality (smoking, drugs and other "cool" behavior). He knew he had enough strength to stand alone. What is interesting is once he stood firm, others joined him.

The intensity of peer pressure depends upon your personal strength of character and values. If we adhere to peer pressure, we may end up sleep-walking through events in our lives. Do we need social acceptance? Yes! We have to follow the rules and laws of the public. We need to be aware of the social and ethical norms of our community and our professional lives to function, while still remaining true to ourselves.

When you step out of the crowd and become an individual, make sure you have evaluated the risks and probable end result. Why wait for the wake-up call (experiencing a significant life event such as divorce, a death in the family or getting fired) to experience a need for change? Evaluate whether nonconformity is for you.

It's a process, not an event.

Speak Up...
I Can't Hear You!

It was the perfect evening for doing exactly what I didn't want to do—attend a business banquet and sit at a table with a bunch of strangers. All dressed up in glitter, dangling earrings and high heels and faced with three hours of small talk. No planned program, just a meal and polite interaction.

Made my day.

Putting on a cheerful façade, my husband and I introduced ourselves to the group. A few muttered responses rose up from bowed heads, along with a feeble attempt at a handshake. Not a very auspicious start. It took about four minutes to cover the other

introductions and discuss the forthcoming meal.
Two hours and fifty-six minutes left and our topic
pool had already run dry.

Time to pull out all the stops. In asking about
their children and requesting a viewing of any family
photos, blank stares greeted our request. I discovered,
if only I had looked a little closer, that everyone at
the table was old. Not old as in white hair and
dentures, old as in having grown-up children who
had moved out and lived on their own. No cute
family photos, just a collective relief at being empty-
nesters. Two hours and forty-five minutes to go.

We were making progress.

Seeing my opportunity to regroup, I excused
myself to the powder room. No other female offered
to join me. What was I thinking? They would have
had to talk to me. Looking closely in the mirror, I
considered replacing my glasses with my John
Lennon-style, opaque wire-rimmed sunglasses and
re-entering the dining area assuming a celebrity
pose. If that didn't encourage a comment....

* * * * *

That's when I realized how far we have removed
ourselves from the art of small talk or "chatting."

I believe several reasons exist as to why people do not participate in social banter when faced with similar situations. Exposing our lack of social skills or creativity can alienate the people we wish to impress, so we remain quiet. Others prize their privacy. They may be forced to attend the event, but they'll be damned if they have to participate. Many may prefer to dismiss irrelevant chitchat and focus their energy on speaking with career peers on work-related issues. Finally, a few simply don't care what others think and prefer to be alone with their thoughts.

Fine.

Get ready to have your space invaded. I've discovered that the simple art of chatting with a total stranger unveils wonderful insight. We can't get to know each other unless we communicate. Interaction builds trust and develops relationships that can be built upon for the future. The existence of this positive contact can defuse tense situations. Through the course of discussion, you can learn a great deal about the other person: their background, life philosophy, common interests, sense of humor, ethics and values. The sharing of hopes and dreams often results in other connections that will help you personally and professionally. To

assist you in enhancing your small-talk skills,
consider some of the following suggestions:

- Demonstrate your wit. You may discover others
  who share your sense of humor.
- Compliment others sincerely and accept
  compliments graciously.
- Talk to people in elevators. Even better, try
  turning around to face the riders. If you're not a
  hit, at least you'll know it right away!
- Ask open-ended questions from everyone you
  meet. Instead of asking "Are you having a good
  day?" where they can simply answer "Yes!", try
  asking "What good things are happening for
  you today?" This will reveal a whole new level
  of information.
- Wear something unusual—lots of color or
  possibly a hat—something that would tend to
  draw out a response. Remember, the reaction
  may not be what you expected, but that is what
  makes the process so interesting!
- Spend a couple hours speaking with kids under
  age seven. They have opinions and insight on
  everything.
- In the middle of a lengthening silence, toss a
  question or statement casually out into the
  middle of the discussion. "Has anyone ever choked
  on a grape?" might be a good place to start.

- Attend networking and social events with the goal to learn something new about three people. It will help you through an awkward time until you locate someone you want to chat with, and it certainly makes time fly.

Next time, if I am faced with having dinner with Mount Rushmore stone sculptures, I'll consider my sunglasses...then return to the table. I wonder if anyone will notice and say something. Hmmmmm.

Getting off the Curb

In my family, I grew up with pre-established concepts and guidelines. We had only two options—either accept the rules or suffer the consequences. No discussion. No gray—just plain black and white. If we made the wrong choice, the family game rule didn't allow us to pass "GO." All children went immediately to jail—regardless of the reasons why we broke the rules. We became excellent Monopoly players, learning at an early age that every action had a reaction, and we unconditionally accepted the consequences for our decisions.

Several years ago, I had the opportunity to travel and assist another insurance branch office with staffing issues and workflow. The managers requested that I interview a woman, who was by far the most unique person I've ever encountered. I entered her cubicle, and there she sat—sunlight glinting off the wide-brimmed tin foil hat perched atop her head. The petite brunette hunched over her keyboard earnestly typing, ignoring the flapping and crackling of the foil folded intricately around her arms. Sensible pumps had shredded the tin foil encasing her feet and produced unsightly fringing.

Stunned, I inquired, "Why tin foil?" She answered quietly, "Microwaves." The company had recently installed a microwave oven for its employees. As a new appliance, the public feared that their overall health might become endangered due to microwaves pelting their immune systems. Upon discovering the placement of this con-troversial equipment on her floor, this lady truly believed that she'd be harmed if she did not protect herself.

Her options left her feeling trapped. On the one hand, she loved her job, but on the other, she was terrified of the ill effects that the microwave could have on her health. In order to remain employed by the company she loved, she felt she had to wear the tin foil suit. Now, you may ask why the company kept her. Her typing speed averaged about 100 words per minute with no errors. After my enlightening interview, management relocated the microwave, and she removed the tin foil. Everything reverted back to normal. This employee stepped out of the crowd after analyzing her risks. She stayed true to herself and her perceptions. What a risk she took!

Once others notice us, we're placed in jeopardy. You know as well as I do that we can't control others' reactions to our appearance, performance or personality. Everyday, I see people modifying their looks, stifling their ideas and burying their personalities so deep that they live in shadows. Does obscurity provide safety? Should we perceive standing in the shadows as bad? Not at all! But, don't complain when promotions or accolades are showered on others and not on you.

Losing one's self in the crowd can ultimately cause us to lose sight of who we are or how we think. We eventually become anesthetized to the ebb and flow of life. Why hide internally while operating on autopilot? Breaking this personally imposed prison of self-doubt and insecurity requires one thing: we must believe in our own value.

Ouch! Did I strike a nerve? Do you feel the electricity of awareness? This sensation may shock you at first. But once you begin to recognize the cause of this newfound energy, you'll do everything in your power to experience it again.

START WITH 15 SIMPLE STEPS

1. Say "NO" more often and don't let others make you feel guilty.
2. Respect your right to have an opinion.
3. Enforce and reinforce personal ethics and values.
4. Commit to your beliefs and be prepared to act on them.
5. Remain flexible, as change is inevitable.
6. Give yourself permission to be emotional.
7. Learn from your mistakes.
8. Vocalize feelings.
9. Build positive relationships.
10. Eliminate yourself as your own worst enemy.
11. Focus on what you do well.
12. Allow others to help you.
13. Offer assistance to others.
14. Share your talents with your community.
15. Play.

Once you stop expecting recognition from others and live your life valuing your contributions and abilities, you'll gain the freedom to be you.

Your friends, peers and co-workers will see you for who you are.

Life becomes clearer. Everyone will know the definition of you, and you will feel more honest with yourself.

TEACH YOUR CHILDREN WELL — AND ALSO LEARN FROM THEM

If You're Not Careful...
You'll Raise the
Perfect Underachiever

G ently replacing the phone back on the hook, I reflect once again how things did not turn out like my husband and I had anticipated. We have a nice, newly furnished home centered on a manicured lawn, comfortable income and lucrative careers that will help us in our retirement, which waits right around the corner.

We would gladly give it all up if we could help our twenty-three-year-old child live up to his potential. Unfortunately, we have already laid down the pattern, making it difficult to design something new. Now, as a legal-aged adult, our son holds the directions for his future.

As parents, we have become bystanders.

The birth of our child gave us unlimited hope for the future. We based our financial decisions upon how they would improve the well-being of our child and family in the long run. Because of frequent job relocations, my husband and I purposely did not establish strong community ties. We didn't understand that our child invested all his energies into making friends in the grade-school level. We didn't see his friendships tear apart time after time after each move.

I finally understood what each move cost our eight-year-old son when we loaded the moving van, preparing for the transfer to Kansas City, Missouri. While living in Pittsburgh, Pennsylvania, Ben became inseparable with David, a small blonde-haired boy, half the size of my son, exploding with energy and gusto. That Saturday, David, feet dragging, wandered over to hand Ben a farewell gift—a small toy.

What stood out about this meeting overwhelmed me. The unforgettable look of sadness on Ben's face as he accepted the parting gift, reflected the fragileness of childhood friendships. He knew he would never see David again.

Quiet amplified the absence of their future friendship with regret and longing.

Ben never complained. He held tightly onto the toy for his entire ten-hour trip. He slept with it and carried it in his backpack to school as a constant reminder of his second-grade friendship that would never flourish into anything but a childhood memory.

We told ourselves that our son had learned how to adapt to new environments and had discovered the art of effective networking. Military families did it and survived...why couldn't we? Our adult logic simply soared over the head and heart of our young child. Stability held no presence in his life—only change.

Our standards regarding Ben's school academic performance remained high. We continued to demonstrate to our son the benefits of hard work. Long hours of work on our part necessitated extended day care or latchkey for Ben. We convinced ourselves that "in the future" we would benefit from sacrificing some of our family time in order to provide financial benefits. We taught Ben the importance of our family unit and that he could rely upon us. Daily, we showed him how much we loved and supported him by attending all his personal events. "Life discussions" over a medium-sized pepperoni pizza became a quiet haven for us to touch base and help him adjust.

Since his birth in 1979, our family has lived in

eleven homes in six different cities. Ben quickly discovered that each new location provided an opportunity to recreate himself. We were unaware of Ben's belief that life offered no outside security. He abandoned any long term plans or relationships, knowing they would only result in emotional hurt.

Ben learned all of this in silence.

We, the ever-busy, self-involved parents stood oblivious to his loneliness. As a family, we built a strong foundation, but didn't acknowledge that it held his only stability. He never truly found himself in a predictable and safe social environment. He buried his self-image in order to conform.

"Effective networking" came to mean giving in to peer pressure. If Ben chose to adapt quickly, he adhered to the rules and established himself in the pecking order. He eventually learned that if he did nothing to bring attention to himself, he could get along. If he dropped out of the Talented and Gifted programs, the mainstream kids would no longer tease him for his intelligence. He buried his academic potential to gain the short-term rewards of social integration. Ben needed to survive in the present and eliminate his loneliness.

To ensure his position within his peer group, Ben submerged his identity and accepted the group rule—that is until it collided with his ingrained value system. At that point, he made a decisive choice to reaffirm his ethics by refusing to play "Follow the Leader." By challenging the status quo, Ben segregated himself socially. This mental war took the light out of our child's eyes. To this day, he struggles in balancing isolation with socialization.

• • • • •

How do we teach our children to be true to themselves? Help them to recognize that peer pressure exists and thrives. Once we, as parents, identify this for ourselves, then we can teach our children this critical life lesson. You need to qualify your level of play within the game of life.

Parents, accept the priority of your children. *We have only one chance to get it right.* As parents we need to be aggressive in centering our children. Teach them how to make choices consistent with a positive self-esteem. Urge them to take appropriate action when necessary, reinforcing their value systems.

This generation of children needs our help more than ever before—just read the headlines.

Eliminate the underachiever by helping your children feel comfortable in their own bodies, minds, spirits and decision-making abilities. Allow and encourage them to express a difference of opinion. Teach negotiation by exploring alternatives that satisfy both family and child. Ready yourself to face conflict when your children challenge parental decisions. At this juncture, the type of family environment you create is critical: it may be one where the child withers from rigid rules or one where he thrives on standards established through mutual consideration.

Parents have to make tough choices. Experience the ultimate achievement by positively guiding your child's development. Evaluate your child's situation. Experience life through your child's eyes and don't be afraid to communicate. You've already survived the wilderness of your own childhood. Your children count on your wisdom.

Let's Pretend

My parents did not believe that their parental duty entailed providing entertainment. Television, a huge jump in technology, dominated and captivated our family living room. No Play Stations or video games, computers or other high-tech devices rested on our shelves. Even if those playthings did exist, our middle-class family of five children with two sets of twins, two years apart, didn't have the financial resources to buy a battery of toys.

We learned to create adventures using our imaginations, making the best of our situation. Visualize a group of kids reading shared stacks of comics while lying on a warm family driveway for hours on end...or crazily jumping out of soaring swings pretending to fly. We narrowly escaped broken bones or bruises—well, maybe not the bruises.

Growing up, our side yard had an enormous willow tree with many outstretched branches that beckoned us to climb up and take a wild ride. Our fertile imaginations saw not just a climbing tree, but a dinosaur tree. The tree had a phenomenal branch that extended out just like the neck of a brontosaurus! We mounted that dinosaur, with a rope bridle in hand, and rode endlessly on its neck. Our mom simply let us be kids, crossing her fingers in hopes that we wouldn't be bucked off in all the excitement.

What a sight for those passing by! I just bet they stared at us with skeptical looks, wondering why those giggling, overactive children were so amused. There we sat having the time of our lives, straddled on this dinosaur neck with our long legs dangling down, moving in every which way.

As children, our parents encouraged us to dream and built a foundation for us to feel good about standing apart from others. Looking back on our dinosaur tree, we had an abundance of willow limbs to choose from; we chose the one that suited us at that particular time of our lives.

• • • • •

Have you gone out on a limb lately? Maybe it's time to swing to another branch of your own dinosaur tree. As Nietzsche said, "The truly mature man is one that has recaptured the seriousness of a child at play." Do you remember how to play?

As an eighth grader, my sister K.C. once brought home a portrait she had painted in art class. That afternoon, my sister proudly presented her school art assignment to Mom, who proceeded to find it a place of honor at the top of the hallway stairs. She hung it immediately and stood back to get the full effect. *Definitely "A" material! Such a talented girl!* As Mom stood there in awe, she noticed that the portrait had no facial features. The painting depicted a front head and shoulder pose of a girl draped in black with long dark hair cascading past her shoulders.

No eyes, mouth—nothing.

That following Sunday, just before the church service ended, Mom, perched in her position in the family pew, noted my sister, a choir member, as she filed directly up the aisle to the back of the sanctuary. As K.C. walked closer towards Mom's vantage point, something made Mom pause and lean forward for a better look—the way K.C. walked with her head down with her long straight hair framing her face, wearing a black choir robe.

The portrait.

After my mother arrived home, entering through the side door, she hung up her coat and headed towards the stairway.

There it was, staring her in the face. It was the portrait—K.C.'s self portrait.

"Oh my god. She's depressed!"

Mom rationalized that K.C. was feeling neglected since she had three new sisters and a brother—two sets of twins, two years apart—for siblings. As the twins grew older, more attention needed to be given just to keep order in the family. K.C. was probably expressing her sadness of being left out of the lime light she had enjoyed for seven years before my twin brother and I joined the family. Concerned for my sister's well being, and trained as a psychiatric registered nurse, mother knew she needed to pay close attention to K.C.

During the parent-teacher conference scheduled a week following Mom's diagnosis, she reviewed K.C.'s art work with her instructor. He pointed out the solemnity of her portrait assignment. Noting his affirmation of her suspicions, Mom had to get to the bottom of what was so severely impacting her daughter.

Mom needed to take action.

Perhaps, if she asked the right questions, Mom could uncover the root of her daughter's melancholy. That evening, she motioned K.C. to the kitchen for a private talk. She initiated a mother-daughter chat by asking leading questions concerning how my sister felt and how she was doing in school with her classes.

Not getting anywhere, Mom grew frustrated and kept trying to discover why K.C. felt depressed. She received no cooperation. K.C. stared blankly at Mom, clueless, not understanding the reason for all the attention.

Exasperated, Mom blurted, "Why doesn't the girl in the painting have a face? Are you depressed?"

K.C. shrugged. "Mom, I can't paint faces! What's the big deal? It was the only way I could get an 'A' on the project."

No depression here. She had simply used her creativity to cover up her lack of training.

●　●　●　●　●

Change can often have a serious impact. Overreaction, before all the research is done, can be just as devastating. If my mother had simply asked the important question right away, rather than jumping to conclusions, the anxiety levels would have been significantly reduced.

K.C. lost a portion of her naiveté that day. She found that others would judge her by the simplest of her actions. Her imaginings and unfiltered outlook on life began to shift.

As small children, we innately knew how to dream. Maybe not paint, but we could dream. Our aspirations are often shoved into the background as we mature.

Re-awaken your dreams. Release your inhibitions. Paint! *Even if you don't know how to draw faces....*

The Bug

If there's one thing I can't stand, it's bugs.

I hate the way they look, the way they walk and the way they creep up on you in the middle of the night. Bugs have a tendency to fly in your face while you're taking a walk around the neighborhood, or they dive bomb into your food at the most unlikely time. My fear of insects began as a small child. We lived in northeast Iowa, where summers were unbearably humid. For about two weeks out of the year, hordes of Box Elder bugs would swarm over the doors, windows and walls of all the area homes. These insects, each approximately a half-inch long, have wings with black and orange colored bodies. They resemble huge lightning bugs without the rear navigational light.

My brother, sisters and I performed various methods of acrobatics in avoiding these bugs to gain entry into our home. If you're wondering if my parents knew about a product called Raid, they did. Even though we maintained regular pest control service, the bug count remained constant.

My husband and I took up residency in Kansas City, Missouri in 1990. We moved from a very temperate Pennsylvania climate where the largest bugs we experienced were small ants. We purchased a soaring two-story style home in a lovely sub-division in Blue Springs, Missouri.

The only downside? Roaches.

In Missouri, roaches are commonplace. Even Mr. Clean wouldn't have been able to avoid having these uninvited guests in his house. These insects thrive in the rocks, in trees, under the sod, in your garbage and inside houses. It requires a concen-trated effort by the owners to clear out the bugs from their residences.

And clear them out we tried.

For six months, we would have the Orkin man show up and spray the house for bugs. The first time they went through the home, they killed a nest of Black Widow spiders, about forty roaches (that were at least an inch in length), and a few Brown Recluse spiders. This spider is very small, has a light brown shape of a violin on its back, and when it bites, its poison degenerates human flesh, melting the skin away.

Great. Just what I needed for a secure state of mind.

After six months, my husband had to go out of town for a few days. No longer would I have the "advance guard" for the roach patrol. The roach patrol in our house consisted of my husband Rick and my son Ben (who was eight years old at the time), creeping up the stairs in front of me, searching for any roaches that might have escaped us during the day. The roaches were most commonly spotted on the master bedroom ceiling. My husband and Ben used brooms, fly swatters or whatever handy weapon they could find to exterminate the roaches before we retired to bed.

After months of having this live-in bug patrol around, I felt fairly secure that an invasion would not occur while Rick was gone.

Boy, was I wrong!

That evening, after my son had been asleep for about an hour, I slowly walked up to the master bedroom to prepare for bed. I scanned the master bedroom ceiling, hoping to confirm the absence of roaches. I slipped into my robe while advancing to the master bath area for my face-washing ritual.

As my paranoia mounted, I made the mistake of looking up. Where the ceiling and the wall joined there hung a large brown roach. When I say large, I'm not just talking large. It was HUGE. It would have been considered fat in the roach community. I'm sure it had survived several years of perils through metropolitan bedroom community living. It just hung there and stared at me.

My heart leapt into my throat, and I backed away. I didn't even want to turn off the faucet. I let the water run. I felt that if I did anything to disturb the quiet for that roach, it would come after me. As I stared overhead, I realized that I alone would have to slay this monster. I had to be the grownup.

Well, this grownup fled down the flight of stairs into the kitchen. I slid across the wood floor, snatched up a broom and raked through the pantry searching for the huge can of Raid insecticide. Clutching my weapons in hand, I marched steadily back up the stairs into the war zone.

I would have worn a helmet if I had one.

Unfortunately, my eight-year-old's football helmet didn't fit!

I stepped into my husband's wingtip shoes. I needed shoes that could crush an elephant. I needed shoes big enough so I couldn't hear the bug screaming and crunching when I laid my vengeance upon it. I needed shoes big enough so I could leap out of them without untying the laces once I dispatched the creature.

I climbed up onto the vanity, never taking my eyes off the roach. I held up the large can of Raid, and made sure the nozzle pointed in the right direction. Saying a soft curse under my breath, I pressed the nozzle of the insecticide can.

I had never realized that the spray shot out in the form of a heavy mist rather than a direct stream of poisonous bug killer. I succeeded in hosing insecticide in my eyes, up my nose, down my throat and onto my skin. I nearly fell off of the vanity into the bathtub. Scrambling down to the floor, I splashed water in my eyes and re-brushed my teeth, sneezing the entire time.

I tentatively looked up and saw the gigantic roach, totally unaffected by my first attack. Time to bring out the big guns.

Grabbing the broom, I advanced again upon the roach. Taking up my place on top of the vanity and straddling my husband's sink area, I prodded the

broom viciously up towards the ceiling intending
to smash the roach...damn—three feet short. I only
succeeded in scratching the wallpaper and making
the roach laugh.

I knew it was laughing at me. It was too big and
old not to have seen everything. This roach knew
that it was safe in its spot. I retreated back to the
bathroom floor. I flung the useless broom into the
master bedroom. Forty-five minutes had passed. It
was time for me to go to bed.

I switched to Plan B: have a good defense rather
than activate an offense. I proceeded to spray the
walls with Raid around the entire perimeter of the
bathroom, reaching up as high as I could. I
determined that the roach had no choice but to be
frozen in his spot as long as the light was on. I
sprayed around the doorway to the master
bedroom and across the floor. I covered the carpeting
around the perimeter of the bed, just to make sure.
As a last measure of security, I sprayed the entire
top of the bedspread.

I clamored into bed and congratulated myself
on how well I had taken care of the situation. In
the middle of a small chuckle, I suddenly recalled
a conversation with a local hospital nurse. She had
delighted in telling me that over 50 percent of
foreign objects removed from human ears were
roaches. Often, the roach was still alive when it

was removed. Something about the warm ear canal seemed to attract roaches.

Convulsing with disgust, I squeezed the pillow over my ears. I felt fairly secure that I would be safe for the evening since I had sprayed the walls, the floors and the bedspread, until I remembered—roaches fly. My nemesis could evacuate his position on the ceiling and simply soar over to my bed and crawl in my ear. If he couldn't make it, I imagined he was assembling the troops.... Into his roach walkie-talkie he would bark his orders: "Roach One to Roach Two. Target has climbed into bed. Once pillow slides from ear, advance. Repeat—advance. I will act as backup, since my position has been compromised!"

Needless to say my evening sentry duty passed fitfully.

The alarm sounded at 5:30 AM. I approached the master bath and stealthily rounded the corner. Target spotted. Position maintained.

With an eye on the roach at all times, I prepared for the day and then went downstairs after waking my son. He took off for school, and I left for work, hoping all day that the roach would be gone when I got home. When I retired to bed that night, I felt confident that the roach would be gone. I strolled into the master bath and looked up to verify my gut feeling.

I couldn't believe it. The enemy was trenched in! I thought it looked a bit thinner as I'm sure it hadn't eaten all day. I thought I heard a little cough, probably due to the Raid fumes it had been inhaling for the last twenty-four hours. There was no way I could sleep that night until that damn bug was eliminated. I called for backup. I roused my son—my brave, confident eight-year-old son—and guided him into the bathroom. He shuffled in his Spiderman slippers while rubbing the sleep out of his eyes with a small hand.

I started my orders with "Ben, I need your help. Do whatever you and Dad do to get rid of this bug on the ceiling! Kill it!"

He looked at me and shrugged, "Sure, Mom."

Ben stepped up to the vanity (which was about chest high on him), stretched out and hit the wall with an abrupt thud. The roach fell to the floor on its back and my son stomped firmly.

Mission completed in less than three seconds.

• • • • •

As adults, we seem to think that we are the wise ones. Growing older gives us a badge of accomplishment and knowledge that children can't even begin to understand. And as we mature, we overlook something quite elementary—common sense.

His approach was uncomplicated—the opposite of my adult approach. He evaluated the easiest route to get his objective accomplished in the most efficient way—he created a small earthquake to dislodge the roach.

The next time you feel the inclination to overlook a statement or suggestion made by your small child, I suggest you listen. They just might have a gem of an idea waiting to be implemented. They just might provide you with your own earthquake that will help resolve a personal problem. Not all of our problems are earth shattering. Simple solutions versus the complex approach may just be the solution you searched for. Trust your instincts and learn from others.

When you are ready to face battle the next time, remember how Ben would handle the situation.

Keep it simple.

ACCOUNTABILITY

High Hopes

My niece and nephews attended Iowa State University. As is the case at any college, students walk into a totally new environment of study habits in retrospect to their K–12 careers. They had a comfort level in high school that placed them in high esteem with peers and administration. Skimmed from the melting pot of high-school students and melded with other top performers, they soon found themselves immersed in a fierce cauldron of international competition for recognition of academic achievement. Marcus, Michael and Lauren, faceless students in a crowd identified only by a social security number, stepped up to bat in a whole new ballgame.

Anticipating their first series of grades, which would then define them in the eyes of the professors in either a negative or positive light, they all became extremely anxious about their final scores. My sister, K.C., was at the receiving end of some soul-searching phone conversations in the late evening hours. She knew her children were by nature high achievers, perfectionists and performance-oriented individuals and understood that their home provided a safe island to vent anxiety.

K.C. would answer the phone for all three children, pacing the living room as she listened to their various issues. In response to each concern, she suggested that they take a deep breath and think.

"Look back at what you did last semester. Did you choose to go out and weight lift, golf or have coffee with friends rather than attending a study group? Did you decide to watch a DVD for an hour-and-a-half rather than prepare for your test?"

They all professed that they took time off as needed, so they wouldn't feel overwhelmed. By taking a breather, they were refreshed and able to attack their studies with a clear mind and outlook. None of the kids expressed regrets in how they handled their first semester.

"If you feel you did the best you could, then don't beat yourself up about your grades," K.C. advised. "You did the best you could do. You're in a whole new environment. If you decided to do something other than study, then you better step back and analyze what you need to change to improve your standings for next semester."

My sister understood that if you play, you pay! It's as simple as that.

By the second semester, all three became comfortable knowing the simple results of their actions and were skillful at balancing socialization and study. K.C. slept peacefully during that second semester.

Until her daughter, Michael, called.

She contacted K.C. with a request for help in guiding her through a dilemma. Her graduate-level art project creating templates for her print-making class was due the next day. Michael felt she needed a deadline extension. She had con-tacted the professor who felt that she could not accommodate her request. Upset, Michael called her mom.

My niece explained that she had taken it upon herself to elaborate on the project, which resulted in it taking more time than she had initially anticipated. She conveyed to the the professor her need for an extension based upon the complexity of her project.

Michael also divulged that her fingers were cramping up from the long intense period of detailing involved in etching her designs into the template. She was perplexed as to why the professor was not open to the extension.

Insight from Mom: "Michael, I'm going to take this from the professor's perspective. She gave you an assignment. Gave you the due date. It was your decision to expand the project. You should have anticipated the need to schedule more time for the assignment."

K.C. took a long breath. "The responsibility was in your hands. Now you have a decision to make. Either suffer through the cramping, putting in long hours to finish the project on time, or hand it in late, taking a demerit for tardiness with the hopes that she will be lenient and appreciate your initiative of turning a simple project into something that exceeded expectations."

My sister knew this was not what Michael wanted to hear. Her daughter had a choice to make and knew the consequences.

Michael turned in the completed project on time. She stopped trying to manipulate the established system and took responsibility. Accountability is demanding. She stood up to the test.

Responsibility and accountability—two tough principles.

Never What
You Expect...

Sam was interesting. He talked constantly, filled with delightful stories of golfing and college life. Flaunting shoulder length hair, he dressed in jeans and plaid work shirts. Sam's short compact build, enhanced by brawny arms and rugged complexion, showcased his most striking feature—his smile.

As a high-school junior, dating this college man presented my first opportunity to experience a kiss. I prepared for the event. I knew which way I would turn my head and how I would close my eyes. But...it's hard to feel mature when you have a curfew.

Sam didn't seem to mind.

As he stood next to me, I towered over him by a good three inches. Somehow, I had overlooked height adjustments in my calculations for kiss maneuvers. Sam, being ever so diligent, noted the dilemma and shifted up one step so we faced eye to eye.

Brilliant! I knew this was going to be good.

After asking permission to kiss me (which I of course responded to by croaking out "yes!"), Sam turned away from me and reached up towards his face. To remove his gum? Such a thoughtful and mature man!

Sam turned back to face me. His teeth were missing! No gum. Sam had slipped out his dentures and tentatively held them in his hand. He looked a bit like Gabby Hayes or that wrinkled old smoker dude in the anti-smoking magazine ads.

Sam made his move.

Leaning back, I stuttered, "Why in God's name did you take your teeth out?"

Sam blinked. He proceeded to describe his Vietnam tour of duty. During an advance maneuver, he and his buddy were placed in "point" position. His friend stepped on a landmine, which resulted in a piece of shrapnel driving its way into Sam's mouth, fracturing his teeth. He owed his smile to dentures and plastic surgery.

Gum chewing loosened the denture cream. Uncertain about their stability, he removed his teeth, rather than having them slip and interrupt the kiss.

That's a good explanation.

However, I couldn't resist asking him, "What did yah think I was gonna do? Suck your teeth out?"

Getting through the laughter, we had our first kiss. With teeth.

By removing his dentures, Sam took a chance. Would I complete the kiss?

He knew his actions were full of risk. But so were loose dentures. Being an accountable and responsible man, he selected an option and understood the possible consequences. For me, it became a lifelong memorable event.

· · · · ·

It's a process of discovery that each and every one of us has to pass through to understand the impact of our decisions on our future, family and dreams. Where does responsibility begin and end?

Only you hold the answer.

BE
PROACTIVE

Checkmate

"*Winning isn't everything, but wanting to win is.*" Vince Lombardi succinctly stated that our mind-set is critical to our position in life. Humans are competitive creatures holding the innate will to win. We flock to cosmetic counters that display lotions and potions intended to make us look younger, thus aiding us in winning the battle against age. We join health clubs and go on fad diet programs. Designers develop wardrobes for the populous, displaying illusions of fitness, status or interests.

Ultimately, we compete to win approval. No one wants to come in second or third place, or for that matter, last. They are the forgotten soldiers who society judges as coming up short.

Making changes in our lives may not be easy, if we don't believe in it. We've stalemated ourselves before the games even begin.

* * * * *

As a recently hired supervisor in a metropolitan area, I had the responsibility for managing approximately thirty people. These individuals had been rushed through the hiring process by upper management due to explosive sales of a new product. One of the new female computer technicians showed up for work and plopped down at her station, completely displaying all of her feminine assets to the entire department. I found it imperative to address the situation immediately.

I summoned her into my office, sat her down and asked, "What position did you hold prior to working here?" She revealed that she had been self-employed. I inquired as to where she educated herself regarding computer technology, and she explained that she was the single mother of a three-year-old and attended local technical computer classes. I then pointed out that she needed to adapt her sitting posture, as well as her mode of dress, to the workplace.

Sensing her comfort and willingness to adjust to her profession, I asked her if she owned clothes that would be better suited for this work environment. She confirmed she had extra spending money and accepted my offer to assist her in shopping for a professional wardrobe.

We set a time to meet downtown Saturday morning. After dropping her child at day care, she showed up with a purse stuffed full of money. We spent the day getting her hair colored and fashioned into a stylish bob, toned down her make-up and shopped for her new professional attire.

Talk about a total makeover! She metamorphosed into a class act. Monday morning, as I watched out of my office, she made her entrance. No one recognized her. She had changed their perception of her. She accomplished her ultimate goal of gaining and maintaining the respect of her child and her peers. She knew this would require internal changes as well as external. She wanted to win and she knew she had to accept change and find her role model. Eventually, she became a role model as manager of her own department.

So…if you update your clothing, sit differently and alter your hairstyle, the world is yours, right?

Not so fast!

Unfortunately, no easy fixes occur for me, as is often true for others as well. Achieving my version of success requires dedication, hard work and outside support. I've struggled through one problem after another. No one can dampen my spirit or stomp out my fire.

Only I'm allowed to do that. And I can be quite effective at this, thank you.

I open my arms to suggestions, encouragement and plain old support. I become rejuvenated each time I take a step closer to my goals. I just keep going and going, like the Energizer Bunny... except I don't run out of batteries. My power source comes from my family, friends and peers. They encircle me with enthusiasm, constantly nudging me forward.

While participating in the process of reaching goals, we cross paths with others who struggle right along beside us. Camaraderie forms and recognition of our common circumstances offers us an opportunity to lend a helping hand. Company can relieve us of our temporary misery. Empathy, understanding and assistance shared by others furnish us with renewed vitality to continue striving for the brass ring.

We enter this world alone and we leave it alone. To thrive during your adventure requires interaction with others. It takes two to tango.

Giving insight to your mistakes or pitfalls invigorates self satisfaction as well as uncovering possible solutions to your own predicaments.

Why should you help others? Because. Because why? I won't leave you hanging with that standard parental retort—that offers no logical reasoning.

Because...you expand your character, knowledge and impact on society. You get involved in something outside yourself. We all leave ripples on the surface that impact people's lives. It's up to us to determine the size and shape of the ripple we initiate. Get out of isolation by extending your hand. Recognize how others have reached out to you. This gesture either shows an offer of help...or relays the need for help. Whatever the interpretation, interaction is accomplished.

Stop playing king of the mountain. Be generous with your expertise. Bend down and pull others up to help them reach their dreams. Having them stand beside you assembles a support system that will help you maintain your balance on the way up.

Generosity makes everyone winners.

Surviving Your Career

I'm at a meeting, but I'm not listening. I look attentive, even involved. But all that broils through my mind is how close my friend David came to losing his job at fifty years of age. In the last corporate downsizing episode, David's family security was threatened—not just financially—and his personal esteem plummeted. More disturbingly, he didn't understand why he was in jeopardy in the first place. David prided himself on his diligent performance and attention to detail, and he faithfully relocated wherever he was needed in his twenty-year career. David believed his company valued his efforts—until the merger.

His company, purchased by a newer "hip"

competitor, completely reorganized all personnel. Turmoil surged in every department as uncertainty grew regarding how the new owners conducted business.

A disregard of the traditional hands-on manner of doing business became apparent in corporate directives. The face to face business David fostered over a twenty-year period skidded to a halt. High technology superceded the need for high touch relationships. Corporate management preferred non-interpersonal ways of building customer/client relationships through phone, fax or internet. Why waste company funds by driving out to meet with the client?

Directives regarding profitability implemented new procedures and techniques. The corporate focus centered on gaining new customers rather than nurturing the existing ones. David reacted as though a bucket of ice water had been dumped on him. His territory had expanded to one of the largest and most profitable precisely due to his "down home" sales technique.

Rationally, David knew that the directives would enhance rather than compromise his effectiveness in customer service. He feared change. Over the years, he had developed and maintained a bond of face to face trust and friend-ship with his clients. He worked his territory with self control and diligence. David developed a sense of daily freedom. He perceived the change as stifling his independence by trapping him in an office from nine to five.

His concerns needed to be addressed. Surely, this new management understood the fragility of customer/representative relationships. David expressed his apprehension during a meeting he scheduled with his vice president. Believing he came from a position of strength, David felt the corporation would recognize and consider his expertise by working with him to gradually integrate the new structure.

Nope. They weren't interested. Everyone had to incorporate the same procedures, which stood as the company's hallmark for success.

Stunned, David realized his position with the company could be in jeopardy. Was he prepared to sacrifice his career to stand behind his convictions?

• • • • •

How does a person prepare for a complete culture change and reorientation of assets and desired skill levels? What was once safe becomes a loaded weapon aimed at economic well-being.

David is not alone in his story.

Frequently, I read about companies downsizing and press releases that emphasize the importance of corporate balance and profitability. Trouble is...the largest cash savings are only possible through the reduction of human capital, facilities and automation.

It's the gut-wrenching realization we get when we learn we're expendable.

The lack of control over situations like this creates fodder for many sleepless nights as you worry over your children's college funds, retirement funds or just paying the monthly bills. You discover multitudes of ways to deal with the stress, from plummeting into self despair, to anger, anxiety, resentment, relief or excitement about the unexpected prospect of building a new, exhilarating career.

So, rather than focusing on ways to self destruct, let's lay down the groundwork to plan for future career opportunities.

SIX WAYS TO CARVE OUT A FUTURE

1.   ATTITUDE
      Eliminate negative thoughts regarding your company's shortcomings. Instead, focus on becoming a linchpin of positive energy and teamwork. Bring concerns or issues to

management's attention succinctly and without condemnation. Provide solutions. Avoid placing your superiors in a defensive stance. I've learned that people tend to push back when cornered.

2.   DELAY GRATIFICATION AND REDUCE DEBT
The significance of the debt Americans accumulate is staggering. Debt eliminates options. It's close to impossible to feel any manner of security when financial liabilities outweigh income (living from pay check to pay check). Loss of income becomes less devastating when you minimize debt—you create room to react responsibly to unforeseen circumstances.

Establish a workable financial plan *now* and begin by creating an emergency resource fund. Try to ignore purchases that are not essential until you have reached your goal.

3.   EDUCATION
Use every opportunity to attend intriguing courses as well as those that provide specific job training for your current position. Consider concentrating on those topics that could develop into careers that would allow you to earn an income in an area you enjoy.

4. UPDATE YOUR RESUME ANNUALLY
    Critically review your performance and achievements by writing them down formally in a resume. Outline your career objectives and evaluate whether your present situation fulfills those ideals. Early assessment of your evolution over the last year may determine a new career direction or alert you to an "at-risk" current position.

5. NETWORK
    Get out and establish meaningful relationships with people in your industry or the field of your choice. In addition, set up informational interviews with businesses that interest you. Prepare for a planned career move either within your firm or to an outside company.

6. FOCUS ON THE TARGET
    Chart the items that you consider important to you—your family, independence, career recognition or net worth? If drawn in three or four different directions, this can be emotionally destructive and reflect in your performance and overall health. Clearly determine your top three priorities and plan accordingly.

Next time when you want to react in a position of turmoil, ask yourself, "Can I afford the consequences?" This question is powerful in its simplicity. Work through your response in a manner that ensures that you stay on track with your true life plan.

Corporate America doesn't owe you a career or a living. So what are you going to do to plan for your future security?

Paper Tiger

As a student, my sister enjoyed being unique, attracted to making her statement to the world—a statement that yelled, "I'm different!" Remember those fringed knee-high moccasins? She wore them before they became popular. Recall the long straight flower-child hair which flowed down in all its glory? She had it. No bouffant for her. The way she moved, spoke and emoted reflected her theater background. I envied her for her pure freedom of expression. But, sometimes expression comes at a cost.

The 1960s proclaimed drug use, political protest and sexual freedom as well as exciting fashion statements. Not much of a radical,

K. C. didn't buy into the first three, but felt it was safe to explore personal expression through clothing.

The fashion industry introduced paper apparel. Clueless, my sister bought into the benefits of owning and wearing disposable dresses—hook, line and sinker. They were advertised as colorful, environmentally safe and as sturdy as Bounty paper towels. She ordered one of the dresses through a catalog that proclaimed it as affordable and disposable. If one were creative enough, she could soak up small spills with the dress invoking the wonders of multiple use!

The package arrived and K.C. eagerly tore it open. After admiring it in the mirror, she knew she had discovered something great—something that would become the envy of her girlfriends and an economic boon to her budget. One late August afternoon, preparing for work, she carefully donned the Kelly-green dress and applied the proper accessories.

She was impressive.

The instructions for the dress were generic and non specific. It was a paper dress. Period. They neglected to tell her that the dress could self destruct.

K.C. had to walk two miles to work that hot, muggy afternoon. Despite the sultry air and scorching sidewalk, her sandals hit the pavement with an assured, confident stride. Until, that is, the dress rebelled.

She stared to sweat...her roll-on deodorant was overwhelmed by the copious amount of moisture accumulating at her armpits. At first, K.C. didn't pay any attention to the situation, until she noticed the dress beginning to thin out at her sides. An unexpected coolness wafted under her arms.

That was when she knew she was in trouble. The confident stride quickly became deliberate. *Must reach work soon!* Her dress was disintegrating.

She focused her entire being on reaching the air-conditioned movie theater where she worked. Exposure threatened. K.C. did not tend toward exhibitionism.

She hustled to her station behind the popcorn counter. Grabbing a stack of napkins, K.C. raced to the ladies room to make the proper adjustments.

Ooops! The dress and napkins clashed.

The napkins, tucked into her bra, flared out from her expanding arm holes like flaps. To keep the napkins trapped and hidden from customer eyes, she clamped her elbows to her sides while serving up the concessions. Adding insult to injury, the heat from the popcorn machine created a recipe for disaster. The air-conditioned haven evolved into her own personal spa. Heat undulated as if it had a mind of its own, threatening to weaken the seams—and you wouldn't believe how rapidly a paper dress absorbs butter.

But K.C. pulled it off—dignity in tact. She excelled in her creativity in reaching for bags, butter and the pop dispenser. Elevated on her toes, swinging her hips, she had moves she never knew she possessed.

Her rescue, activated by our parents, ended the evening. The dress deserved a proper send off: she flushed it down the toilet.

• • • • •

Often, we jump into situations without reading the label and wonder why disaster occurs. Labels are there for a reason.

Common sense took a back seat to individuality. K.C. wanted to do something different, but didn't fully research all possible aspects of wearing a paper dress. She didn't complete her Ben Franklin—her homework. Think before you act.

Ask questions and listen to the responses with an open mind, knowing you may be confronted with the worst case scenario. K.C. lucked out in that she only had to deal with embarrassment. Avoid serious scenarios by asking the right questions at the right time.

Look for the obvious, and read the label—*please*.

MAKE THE BEST OF THINGS, COME WHAT MAY

It's Your Move

Pittsburgh, Pennsylvania, a welcoming city, survived its challenges. Holding a position of Administrative/Human Resource Regional Manager, our parent company, considering financial cuts by way of staff reductions, initiated a meeting with the Pittsburgh branch. My vice president, unexpectedly called out of town, summoned me into his office. I received the assignment of affirming the sound condition of our regional office to two of our top corporate executives.

Perfect for the evening, I slipped into my new blue silk two-piece dress. Navy…a "killer corporate color." Its low "V" back draped down my back, accented by silk buttons, created a stunning effect.

This unique and aggressive dress demanded attention. A perfect diversion.

Dressed to impress, I thought I looked great. Though slightly uncomfortable, I tolerated my tight collar. So what if I had gained a little weight? I was ready to dazzle.

I met them at an exclusive restaurant—a renovated train station from the 1800s, which featured a stained-glass ceiling and sweeping staircase. The perfect background for this critical meeting.

The gray-haired Chief Executive Officer, blessed with patrician good looks, accentuated his presence by donning a pin striped suit coordinated with a crimson tie and matching handkerchief. His gold watch flared in the restaurant lighting. Impeccable. Reserved. Intimidating.

The Chief Financial Officer, on the other hand, exuded a jovial demeanor…approachable. No knee shaking here. As the actuarial for our company, the CFO initiated probing questions, staring intently at me throughout dinner while we discussed our region's status.

Mr. Pin Stripe observed.

Countering the CFO's questions superbly, I glanced up to observe a stunning young lady glide down the central staircase. Elegant in her carriage, I noted her attire.

Wait. That looked like my dress. Except… hers

had a "V" neck.

The room felt hot at that moment, and I reached up to adjust my neckline. This couldn't be happening. Watching the woman's entrance while tugging at my collar, the light bulb turned on. Feeling the label in front confirmed that I had put my dress on backwards.

"Excuse me for a moment...." I muttered to my dinner companions. I hurriedly sought the rest room to check myself in the mirror. A red line gleamed at my throat from the rubbing of my neckline. I stared into the glass.

Stay the way I am? Turn the top around? Uncomfortable, I opted to turn it around.

Laughing and regaining my composure, I spun the top around. Releasing the constriction, my voice lost its croaking quality. Rubbing vigorously, I tried to minimize the red line at my throat.

Now I just appeared a little flushed. In fact, the new "V" neckline flattered me.

Maybe they wouldn't notice.

Returning to the table, the executives' smiles faltered a bit as they welcomed me back. A look of uncertainty passed between them. I ignored it and resumed our conversation. After a period of bated silence, Mr. Pin Stripe, my CEO, Mr. Intimidating, with cocked head on his fist and tongue in cheek, inquired, "New dress?"

He had noticed my "V" back had miraculously transformed into a "V" neck.

Good detail man.

I calmly stated, "No. I just turned the top around. You see, I hadn't realized that this dress was on backwards until I saw the dress on that girl over there. Now, don't get me wrong. Just because I can't dress myself properly, doesn't mean we aren't doing what we can to make sure our operation runs as smoothly as possible!"

They roared! We shared a good laugh about my ability to cope with unusual circumstances. Concise action to eliminate discomfort showed them I had a proactive attitude, not just horrible fashion sense. If you know a situation is wrong... why not just fix it? Don't procrastinate or let a situation get out of control despite the potential for embarrassment. Fix it. It is better than compromising yourself or your company! My honesty and sense of humor made an awkward moment a memorable one.

When was the last time you had the opportunity to correct a mistake, but failed to do so because you might lose face? Next time—turn the dress around!

Strip Plowing

After the first year of marriage, my husband Rick and I moved to a rural community to farm approximately 670 acres of flat, rocky ground in Northern Iowa. Having never had anything to do with farming in my life, I was not prepared for the mind-numbing boredom associated with driving a piece of machinery up and down a field in hot, muggy weather. The sun would shine down relentlessly on the hood of our large red tractor, and the air was still—so still, that a shout faded quickly since it could not gather enough momentum to carry it to its target.

Farm life—oh boy! A dirty, hot, cold, windy, humid, clogging pores type of a living. Forget fashion, all that mattered was the work. And the work never stopped except during the winter calm.

In our first season, I learned how to drive the large tractor and the two-ton truck. Using the gears proved relatively simple and required a bit of coordination to adjust the hydraulics for the plowing equipment, but I felt I was really getting the hang of it. Preparing the fields for planting began the same time as newborn wildlife explored the wonders of the world in early spring. As I drove up and down the fields, I kept an eye out for the hand-sized baby bunny rabbits that would run in the corn furrows in front of the tractor. They never scrabbled out of the furrow perpendicular to the vehicle in order to escape danger. Watching me on the tractor, my husband would just hang his head. There I went again…stopping the tractor, putting it in neutral, leaping out onto the cornfield trying to urge the baby bunny to safety.

The thought of accidentally driving over these innocent babies was just not an option.

To Rick's credit, he never criticized me about it. He just realized that field work would take three times longer than normal if I was at the wheel. So, he planned accordingly. However, that didn't help me much with the boredom. Because Rick knew I was doing the best I could in carrying out the grueling unfamiliar tasks, he decided to be creative.

The field required two people to plow the soil simultaneously in order to make any effective headway for planting preparation. We would drive in large circles, in opposite directions, and meet once a rotation as we passed each other.

After a couple hours at the wheel on a pass one day, I looked up and saw Rick wave at me. Naturally, I waved back. Proceeding with the next rotation, we met again at the turn. I noticed he had removed his hat. Rick waved to me again. I waved back and smiled. On the next turn, as I looked up to greet my husband, I noticed he had removed his shirt. It wasn't that hot, and I didn't mind the view at all, but I thought it was a bit curious. I blew him a kiss. Rick just grinned broadly and roared down the corn row.

With each rotation, as we met going in opposite directions, Rick removed another article of clothing. He'd wave his belt in the air, use his pants as a flag attached to the door, and demonstrate hand puppets with his socks. I couldn't wait to see what else he would do the next time we met. My sides heaved from laughter. Thank God we were miles away from civilization. I kept imagining what his parents would have thought had they driven out to visit us…which wasn't an uncommon occurrence.

Completely naked, Rick then proceeded to put his clothing back on one item at a time for each rotation. His obvious delight at his unexpected prank made the afternoon boredom evaporate. For the next two years, I never approached my work on the tractor quite the same again. I realized that boredom was a state of mind, and I could control that. I could create the source of my own relief. A powerful lesson....

· · · · ·

The choices we make to deliver adventure into our lives dictate how we approach life. Our humor is ours to enjoy, not stifle. Those moments of intense trauma or complete boredom can have their effect dimmed by humor. That day, I learned that you never know what is going to happen or what exciting event might wait around the corner. What outlook on life do you have? Are you confined in boredom and unable to work purposefully to activate your dreams?

Delight in the unexpected.

Godiva Chocolate— Riding Romantic

What is it about romance?

As I grew up and watched movies, I soon learned that the ultimate vision of a romantic encounter happened during a sunlit picnic on a wind swept hillside accented with a beautiful bronzed couple toasting each other with champagne and chocolate-dipped strawberries as the worldly male read softly from a book of love poems....

In novels, I discovered that the heroine always possesses waist-length, glistening, silky hair flowing in sultry slow motion framing her heart-shaped face and full, pouting lips—the type of lips only collagen can produce.

The hero is portrayed as a dashing muscular figure sporting a loose white shirt unbuttoned to the waist. The type of guy who really understands what it takes to make a woman swoon—his intensely focused attention for more than a minute.

That smoldering look. A Latin lover kind of look. Oh, the look. The look that makes a woman's knees melt! It's like the feeling that I get when I'm about to purchase a piece of Godiva chocolate. Decadent, but worth every penny.

To me, the ultimate romantic interlude is the horseback ride on a white sand beach at early dawn. Imagine a large, gray Lipizzaner horse with braided mane, finely-boned face and a proud arch to its neck with its tail fanning outward like a flag. The air is heavy with the smell of jasmine, and the surf beats against the shoreline in time to the pounding of the horse's hooves. The sky shimmers in colors only the tropics can produce.

The color of love.

A woman riding sidesaddle with a loose flowing gown that drapes gracefully off her left shoulder laughs in exhilaration while her hair whips the air behind her—taunting her lover who surges after her riding bareback on an equally elegant steed.

I wanted to live this scenario. For years, I would point out these romantic scenes while reading a book or watching TV…hoping that my husband would get the hint. Rick is the perfect hero for my fantasies. Standing six feet, two inches tall, he wears a red beard like a badge of courage, and his hair is tied back in a stylish ponytail. When he lets it loose, it makes you think about Fabio or Antonio Banderas. In the right setting, he could be transformed!

And all these years, I thought he wasn't listening. Yet, he booked a vacation on the island of Barbados—an isolated island approximately ten miles off the coast of Venezuela and known for some of the whitest beaches in that hemisphere. The temperature, approximately eighty degrees, literally dripped with humidity.

Upon checking into our hotel, my husband noticed that horseback riding excursions were available through the hotel with rides from dawn to dusk. Unbeknownst to me, he made inquiries at the front desk, while I struggled upstairs hauling our three bags into the guest room.

Approximately thirty minutes later—grinning from ear-to-ear—Rick handed me a brochure and a ticket. It was a horseback ride scheduled for one person at 6:00 AM the following morning with complimentary champagne and croissants. Only one slot was open in the schedule, as the rest of the week was booked up.

Since Rick knew how much I wanted to reenact my scenario, he felt it best that I should enjoy that sunrise gallop. He would cheer me from the sidelines trying to look as smoldering as possible as I raced on the beach through the waves.

Morning did not come quickly enough. I prepared my makeup in elegant detail and mussed up my hair for that windswept look. At 6:00 AM, just as the sun peaked over the horizon, Rick escorted me to the back of the resort where he picked up our champagne basket. The swimming pools shimmered in the new dawn light confirming that I would have the experience of a lifetime.

Rick hailed a white-haired, stooped, leathery-skinned native wearing swim trunks, flip flops and a tired, irritated look. He shuffled up to us and asked "Here for the ride, mon?"

I grasped his hand and introduced myself and let him know I was ready for a ride of a lifetime. A dream come true.

"Harrumph..." he muttered. "Get on."

"Get on what? Where is my steed?"

At this point, Rick had retired to a cabana chair clutching the champagne bottle and stuffing a croissant in his mouth. My guide waved his hand at the hitching post behind the stable. I turned to admire my ride. I was stunned to silence.

I thought he was pointing to a big dog at first. I looked closer and realized it was actually a horse. A tired horse—a tired, *old* horse. Growing older by the second. Its coat appeared matted and encrusted with salt stains. Could it have rust? Buzzing black, lumbering flies slowly spiraled up through its nostrils and landed with apparent delight on its encrusted eyes. My steed's back was no longer horizontal—it was bowl shaped, and its ribs poked out painfully with each breath it managed and surged outward as it coughed.

A moist sound erupted from the horse, emitting a foul odor that wafted through the air. A sweat-stained, scuffed halter and saddle invited me to swing up and ready myself for the ride of my life.

"Hop on!" the old man snorted impatiently, pointing dramatically towards the saddle. I turned beseechingly towards my husband. He placed his head between his knees and let go with a fit of laughter that sent little pieces of croissant spewing from his mouth.

I couldn't believe it. This was not the majestic Lipizzaner I had dreamed about! Where was that smoldering look from my lover?

I could either ride the Great Dane-sized horse or I could walk away and never live it down. Well, I was damned if I wasn't going to have my romantic ride.

I inched delicately over to the horse, ran my hand softly across its forehead, and wiped it quickly off on the side of my shorts. A couple of flies came along with it. I easily stepped over the back of the horse and stood. The horse was so swaybacked I could stand up over its back. I sat down. The saddle had no stirrups. To ride this animal and avoid dragging my feet in the sand as we soared up and down the beach, I had to tuck my knees up under my chin and clench them tightly to the saddle horn to avoid falling off.

The horse coughed and gasped for air, causing my knees to blow out to the sides. With a huge sigh, I reached for the reins.

"Can't give you the reins. The hotel rules say that I must lead you up and down the beach during the twenty-minute ride," grunted my guide. Rick had opened the champagne and was hoisting a toast in my direction. His look of utter love was too poignant to describe.

"Let's just go!" I growled through clenched teeth. It was 6:15 in the morning and people had started to wander down to breakfast in the cabana area. A small crowd of people had gathered to enjoy the spectacle of this crazy woman riding a way-too-small horse.

The stable master began to shuffle towards the surf, dragging the horse behind him at a pace so slow, I was stupefied. No wind, just the coughing of the horse. Fifty steps west, fifty steps east, fifty steps west, fifty steps east…. I think the old guy thought the horse would die of exhaustion and wanted to stay near the hotel, just in case. We only went as fast as we did due to the fact that the animal was gas-powered.

As we rounded each turn, my husband would hoist the champagne bottle and yell out loudly, "To your dream, Karel! To romance!" The crowd loved it and applauded me as I passed in front of their tables.

I rode the entire twenty minutes—smiling every inch of the way and flinging my hair to the wind. I waved gaily to each of my admirers—especially to my husband. For him, I had a special salute.

* * * * *

Romance. Life…it's never as advertised. It sneaks up on you through many of life's moments. During that ride, I felt it wasn't fair that I had been cheated that day. I had built such an expectation for my dream, that reality paled in comparison. Afterwards, feeling a bit foolish, I understood. I would never play the role of the heroine. I was just some clumsy woman trying to feel beautiful and pursued.

As weeks went by, I finally understood every-thing. After twenty-three years of marriage, Rick attempted to make a dream come true by purchasing a ticket to ride a beautiful steed on an early dawn morning on an island beach. Without being asked.

The romance came from the purchase of the ticket…not the ride.

Romance is about the moment. Life blossoms in the opportunities that present themselves. True adventure evolves from how we react to life. I no longer feel slighted. I feel loved and honored by his thoughtful kindness.

What dreams do you have in your back pocket? What opportunities are you passing up because they are not exactly perfect?

Find the adventure. Purchase the ticket!

The Scoreboard

As a young adult, I accompanied three other girls on a canoe trip in northern Minnesota. Think of the television ads depicting all that Minnesota offers...nature abounding, loons, moose and serene lakeside vistas. You name it, I saw it. Unfortunately, I'm not a nature lover.

Nature and I mix like castor oil and kids. Insects panic me into performing the fifty-yard dash. I respect and avoid natural water environments because that unknown predator of humans waits just for me. I don't do wooded environments because I guarantee that I'll end up being the main entrée for a bear's lunch. Anything that can go wrong in nature will, if I'm involved.

Why did I go on this trip? Peer pressure. I let it happen. An invitation was extended and like an idiot, I said yes. I tried to be "with it" and thought an opportunity presented itself to break me from my stalemate situation.

No one told me I had to haul a canoe on my head over land to move from lake to lake, or that the only water I'd drink would come from the lake itself—the same place where I'd bathe and wash dishes. On one of those advertised picture-perfect mornings, I became one with nature. We slathered on cocoa-butter tanning lotion and dressed for the trek through the woods to haul our canoe to the water's edge.

Upon arrival, we undressed down to our swim-suits and paddled to the center of the mirror-like, clear blue lake for a leisurely bask in the sun. As we lazily enjoyed the morning's warmth, we heard a low approaching drone. We surveyed the shore-line and spotted a dark throbbing cloud advancing upon us. As it neared, we saw black and yellow colors reflected off the water's surface.

In our exuberance, we forgot one of the camping commandments. In nature, use good *sense* not good *scents*! The smell of the cocoa-butter attracted a swarm of yellow jackets!

Imagine four screaming girls, hurtling into the lake, and flipping the canoe on top of them for protection. We congratulated ourselves for our quick thinking as we heard the bees pelting themselves against the canoe.

That was the end of rational thought.

Under our canopy's protection and amidst our congratulations, we made another mistake. We looked down. Talk about a rock and a hard place. On a bright sunny day, in a clear blue lake, under a turned over canoe, we could see to the bottom of the lake...including all its aquatic inhabitants. We could see their size, shape and teeth. We could see them assessing our predicament.

Our muffled shouts echoed from under the canoe and bounced off the uninhabited hillsides. Ever try to fit up and through an upside down canoe seat?

After what seemed like a lifetime, the bees swarmed off for better pastures. We righted the canoe and quickly paddled to shore. Hurriedly, we climbed into our jeans not realizing that the bees found better pastures in our accessible pants that reeked of cocoa-butter. The stings were relentless.

* * * * *

The process of evaluation and personal growth complicates the game of life. We need to recognize how our changes impact our work environment, family and future. The goal is to score—to achieve emotional freedom. Our life scoreboard equals all of our achievements. We are the controlling factor.

My mother and I were strolling down the city streets of Pittsburgh, Pennsylvania one afternoon, when out of the hustle of city life rose a sound that stopped us mid-step. Pausing on this dreary metropolitan street, we identified the sound of a man's voice—but not just any voice. A resonant baritone, powerful, melodic and true to tone, surged through the city's orchestral din. Mom and I threw questioning glances at each other and listened intently for the source.

A duet was formed—his passion of song combined with the excitement of our search. The voice drew us to a storefront where a man sat in a wheelchair. Even though this street person sat wrapped in tragedy, invisible to the average commuter, I'd like to think he used his talents not only to provide income, but to remind others of his legacy.

His freedom of expression helped me understand that my life music score is as essential to me as his singing talent is to him. His soulful voice still echoes in my memories of Pittsburgh.

How can we begin to take into account what we have achieved in our lives and calculate our own scoreboard? What moments were the most critical and whom have we impacted? Try not to get bent out of shape keeping score. Remember that some games we play are more important than others. Our evaluation is not the mission. Accepting the paths we have chosen and understanding those decisions shape our character.

In our initial evaluation, we may expose bitterness or depression. We must determine if we have control of making a change. If content and satisfied with our lives, we automatically validate our past decisions. It confirms that we probably have chosen the right branch.

Glass half full or half empty...we're labeled as pessimistic, optimistic or complacent by how we perceive that simple illustration. I like to look at it as filled part way. The level of the glass depends upon what changes we have made, what direction we choose and if we need a drink once in a while.

Society habitually classifies us. It determines our status beginning at birth and evolves with every decision we make. Society may block our efforts from even joining the game. Our scores may not end up on the board. We've lost if we accept this judgment.

However, society controls the game as the referee. Our culture determines the rules by which we play. If you challenge society's basic guidelines, prepare for ejection from the game.

The good news is that the scorekeeper wipes the board clean when a new game commences. During each moment of our lives, we get a new chance. We have the ability to zero out our scoreboard and start afresh with a whole new game plan any time we want. Nothing's permanent unless we're convinced otherwise.

Hold yourself accountable and responsible for meeting your own expectations. Eliminate excuses. Want to add color to your wardrobe? Start with the next outfit. Want to own a classic car? Start a savings account, work an extra job and buy it. Want to live in the mountains but your spouse wants to live by the ocean? Find a location that satisfies both of your desires.

It can't be that simple, can it? Sure. It requires a single-minded, proactive attitude, which takes time and a plan. All you need to do is determine the levels of importance.

• • • • •

How will you be remembered? The ball is in your court. Through your persistence and belief, you'll design your legacy.

14 ROUTES TO INSIGHT

- Trust your gut reaction—our innate survival instincts exist for a reason.
- Don't hide emotionally—complacency makes you invisible.
- Learn something new about others—connect on a personal level.
- Direct your energy where appreciated.
- Guard your personal integrity and self respect.
- Stop being a victim of circumstance.
- Ask the right questions—in the right way, at the right time.
- Assume nothing—go to the source.
- Don't be afraid to play—center yourself.
- Life's not fair, so handle it.
- Remain flexible.
- Generosity makes everyone winners.
- Raise the bar of your expectations.
- C.Y.A. = Cleanse Your Attitude.

Getting off the Curb Workbook

GETTING OFF THE CURB

Time to do a "Ben Franklin"—prepare a list of pluses and minuses. Set aside some time for yourself with no distractions in a comfortable spot and prepare to use lots of paper. Prepare for a new game—set up the board.

· · · · ·

LIST THE FOLLOWING:
- Your passions
- What makes you proud
- What you want to achieve
- Activities you enjoy

- Talents you're proud of
- Personal characteristics you want to change
- Type of people you associate with
- Careers you'd love, regardless of requirements
- Your greatest supporters
- Individuals you trust
- People who stop your personal development
- Community work/volunteerism in which you participate

· · · · ·

DESCRIBE IN DETAIL:
- A coach or mentor whose ethics you value
- The rooms in your home that reflect your personality
- The city, state or country in which you want to live
- How others define or perceive you
- Your preferred manner of dress
- The car you'd drive if money were no object
- Your favorite pastimes or hobbies
- Your greatest fear and your greatest success
- Strengths others perceive you have

· · · · ·

By compiling this information, your game plan becomes more evident. Once you locate your starting point, you can map out your future. Pick out those areas you can address. Determine the level of importance in your life and take action if you want to start now.

• • • • •

PROFILE THE FOLLOWING:
- Likes and dislikes
- Strengths and weaknesses
- Career ideal
- Hobbies
- Dreams
- Friends and support system
- Self improvement areas

• • • • •

You have just summarized your wants, needs and the current condition surrounding your life. It's up to you to pull this data together and make it work for you. Put your information in its proper perspective. Get out your mental scale and weigh your options.

• • • • •

RELEASE THE "REAL YOU":
- List your values (i.e. integrity, honesty, etc.). Refer back to your profile to identify those traits

and passions you will incorporate as part of your everyday life.

- Define your personal code of ethics (i.e. how you would behave if your actions would never be discovered).
- Describe the defining moment that has established your code of ethics.
- Describe a situation that created a personal ethical dilemma and how you handled it. Were you satisfied with how it was resolved? If you faced this dilemma today, would your approach be different and how?
- If you change nothing in your life's direction, what's the worst-case scenario? Can you live with it?
- By staying in the same situation and doing nothing, will it cause a decline in your personal health or create undesired turmoil within your family?
- What dreams do you regret not pursuing or what aspirations have you neatly tucked away and forgotten about, due to various roadblocks of life? What derailed your plans?
- When did you first hear "you can't do that anymore"? How did that make you feel?
- Do you like yourself as an adult? Or do you want to regain/recover the qualities you had as a child? What were they?
- Have you balanced your perceptions and desires with reality?

- Describe a course of action where you were met with an unexpected response. How did you handle it?
- Have you faced a situation where the conversation veered to an inappropriate level or where peers treated others unfairly? What did you do?
- Under what circumstances do you now experience peer pressure? Write an example.
- Do you live the life that reflects your values and does your circle of friends share those values?
- Do you want others to know the real you?
- How and why have you modified your looks, ideas or personality? How did this provide security and confidence?
- How can you change your life so that you are playing your game and not someone else's?
- How will others be impacted by your decision to change?
- What do you consider a devastating type of rejection and why would it be devastating to your esteem?
- How do you allow others to make you unhappy? Describe a specific situation. What would happen if you spoke up?
- List three positive actions you will commit to in achieving your success.
- Identify two ways to engage the support of your family and friends in reaching your goals.
- What steps can you take to establish your legacy?

About the Authors

    Karel Murray, founder of Our Branch, Inc., is an accomplished national speaker, motivational humorist, and trainer specializing in topics concerning ethics, motivation, accountability, and sales training. She presents keynotes, concurrent programs, and full day training sessions for business professionals and the general public. The author shares her life with her husband, Rick, son, Ben, and a herd of pets.

TO CONTACT KAREL:
Toll Free Number   866-817-2986
E-Mail   karel@karel.com
Web Site   www.karel.com

K.C. Lundberg's talent and experience drawn from her training as a former English/Theatre educator, women's fashion buyer, a current certified funeral pre-planning consultant, life insurance agent, community volunteer wife, and mother resulted in co-authoring *Straight Talk— Getting Off The Curb* with her sister, Karel.

To order additional copies of

STRAIGHT
TALK

Getting off the Curb

Send $13.95 plus $4.00 S & H
to

Arnica Publishing, Inc.
620 SW Main, Suite 345
Portland, OR 97205

Call 503-225-9900
to order by phone.

Order online at
www.arnicapublishing.com